Little Blasphemies

Little Blasphemies

and Other Observations

David Geiman

WHALER BOOKS

Buena Vista, VA

1 3 5 7 9 10 8 6 4 2

Library of Congress Control Number: 2023919812

Little Blasphemies
David Geiman

p. cm.
1. Poetry: Subjects & Themes—General
2. Poetry: Subjects & Themes—Animals & Nature
3. Poetry: General

I. Geiman, David, 1944– II. Title.
ISBN 13: 979-8-9892186-0-8 (softcover : alk. paper)

Design and Layout by Karen Bowen

Whaler Books
An imprint of
Mariner Media, Inc.
131 West 21st Street
Buena Vista, VA 24416
Tel: 540-264-0021
www.marinermedia.com

Printed in the United States of America

This book is printed on acid-free paper meeting the requirements of the American Standard for Permanence of Paper for Printed Library Materials.

To Steve, who dedicated his life to teaching

Contents

Introduction ix

Mourning Dove 1

Evening Prayer 2

History 3

Father's Dream 4

Thistles 5

The Habitable World 8

The Speed of Light 10

The Black Canyon of the Gunnison 11

Before Poets 12

Trees 14

Zero 16

Sound 17

The Great War 18

Defenseless 20

Atoms 22

Writing 23

A Duty of the King 24

The Big Bang 27

Birdsong 28

The Flight of a Big Bird 29

Deus Ex Machina 30

The Moon 32

The Ark 34

Spring 36

Summer, 1954 37

Autumn 38

Winter 40

Hell 41

Fireflies 42

A Modern Grace at Dinner 44

The True Life of Birds 45

Flight 46

No Square Stars 47

The Last Spy 50

Mozart and Cicadas 51

The Problem with Greek Gods 52

The Smell of War 54

The Bobcat 56

Sennacherib 58

Holofernes 60

The Motorcycle 61

Nineveh 64

French Cicadas 66

Borromeo 68

Mesopotamia 71

Enheduanna 74

Glossary 76

Introduction

I think I have read that there are only five or six poets in the United States who make a living from writing poetry. Given the small number of people who seem to read poetry, that is probably enough. Given that, it is no small effrontery to the Muses that I have written this little volume.

And speaking of Muses, we have to assume that poetry was once much more a part of people's lives, because of the nine daughters of Zeus, the king of gods, and Mnemosyne, the goddess of memory, three of them are Muses of poetry in some manner.

The oldest daughter, Calliope, is the Muse of Epic Poetry in addition to Music, Song, Dance and Eloquence. Erato is the Muse of Erotic poetry. Very busy at that I must assume, since she has no other duties. And finally, Thalia, is the Muse of Comedy and Bucolic Poetry.

In truth, my poems don't really fit into any of the categories favored by the daughters who were the result of Zeus and Mnemosyne's nine uninterrupted days of coupling, and I certainly don't want to irritate them, because when King Pierus of Macedon named his daughters after the Muses, thinking them more beautiful and talented, Zeus turned them into magpies. And while I like birds, I don't want to spend the rest of my days in a tree.

I think I could more accurately say that my Muse is Billy Collins, who writes about daily life and his immersion in it, in a very approachable and friendly, and often comic, manner. So, Zeus, pay attention.

My original idea was to take the themes from a book of personal experiences that I wrote during the Covid years and condense some of the chapters into Haiku or Tanka. That effort ended after one badly composed Haiku. Counting even a short number of syllables is worse than counting sheep, a practice I despise.

After that, the poems just seemed to arrive, stimulated by doubts, epic questions and memories cobbled together over seven decades. I hope you are only mildly offended by any examples of irreverence.

David Geiman, July 2023

Mourning Dove

Does the mourning dove
    Ever waken on a dew-filled dawn
With a clear-faced sun lurking
    Just beyond the horizon
To leak a bit of joy and warmth
    Into a night-addled
Forest of shadow and musk

And say to herself
    This day I will not mourn,
This day I will hold to silence
    As I know no other tune
But one of sadness
    Bleak emotions
And incipient despair

And such a day as this
    Deserves a happier refrain?

Apparently not.

Evening Prayer

God, I just wanted a short word with you
    Before I fall asleep
I know you must be quite busy,
    Up to your ears in
Evening prayers

Which reminds me, that now
    That the earth is round, isn't
Someone saying evening prayers
    Like, twenty-four hours a day?
Or is that why you don't have
    A big franchise in
Central Asia and lots of
    Africa?

Although, I guess you
    Still have to deal with
New Zealand and Australia
    And the Philippines
Since Spain went there a while
    Back with those missionaries

So anyway, now I forget
    What I wanted to ask
And I'm getting sleepy,

Good night.

History

The only time you can look at the sun
    Without going blind
Is at dawn and dusk

So it is with the past sometimes.

You can only know it from a distance.
    The history of the world is
Not a collection of dates
    And merchants' records, no;
The history of the world
    Can not be known
Until the collection of
    Those dates and merchants'
Records and the hidden
    Files of spies and thieves
And an occasional hero,

Reveal the consequences of their deeds.

Father's Dream

How do you get over it,
When you dreamed of rivets
   And bundles of colored
     Wires
Of calipers and lathes and
   Smooth shiny metal,
Of landing gear and blades
   That slice the air.

And you get two old horses,
   Steel wheels and corn planted
On a checkerboard of loam,

Barbed wire, sagging gates
   And rotted fence posts
Oaken stables and
   Sulking cows waiting
To be milked,

Sunday school at ten
   Plodding sermon at eleven
At one the children gather the eggs

And supper on the Lord's Day is
   Always grilled cheese sandwiches.

Thistles

A few decades ago
    In August
When the battle for supremacy
    Over the weeds in the
        Potato patch
    Had long been lost,

Our earthly father
    (not the one residing beyond
        the clouds who seemed to
            have gone on summer break—
        based loosely on the absence
            of answered prayers
        for minor needs)
Would send me to roam
    The pasture, now
Parched and veined by
    Cow paths leading to
The shady spot by
    The garden fence and
        The shallow crossing
            Of the creek
        By the limestone springhouse
That was tumbling rock
    By rock into a useless future,

Where, now bearing mattock
    And a bad attitude
I would set to slowly lay waste
    The errant thistles
And spindly milkweeds,
    Both of which had already
Flowered and let fly on the
    Evening breezes a whole
New generation of
    Asteraceae and
Asclepias Albicans.

My father didn't seem to
    Care that the noble thistle
Was the floral emblem
    Of Scotland and Lorraine.
The same Lorraine that
    Had spawned a forbear,
Minor though he was,
    But essential in the chain.

Nor did he care that that
    Selfsame thistle was the
        Emblem of the great
            Compendium of assembled
        Knowledge of the day,
            The Encyclopedia Britannica.

Even more, he did not know,
    And knowing would not
Have cared,
    That Pliny held that the spiked
Thistle might make the bald
    Head once again grow hair,
Cure the plague and
    Soothe an aching brow.

I will admit to no great
    Love of this prickly plant
Cousin to artichokes
    And Cynara, the
Source of rennet for making cheese,
    But the long fibrous taproot
Of Cirsium, Carduus and Silybum
    Draws energy from the stone-bound
Earth, and in a Trojan gesture
    To the flora it will soon mock,
Lifts life enhancing
    Mineral traces to the hungry
Thankful ranks.

The Habitable World

We should take better care
    Of the small habitable
        World that holds us.
For the truth is
    Humans can only exist
In a two-mile thick
    Shell around a ball
Of shifting magma and a
    Rind of rock and clay.

We cannot descend
    Into the depths like
A worm into an apple
    And find life there.

And even with wings
    We could not soar
To heights above
    Without the hungry
Gift of science and physics.

And these gifts are not free.

We can but rush to and fro,
Like water striders on
The glassy surface of a pond,

And we can look into space
Beyond the stars
And imagine freedom
But we are not free to
Nakedly go there.

The Speed of Light

Even at the speed of light,
    Our souls cannot catch eternity.
It has a jump on us.

And should we, by some
    Miracle wrought by angels,
Exceed the speed of light,
    We must travel backward
In time for counted
    Billions of years to
Join all the elements
    Of the universe as they
Condense into the first dark
    Atom before Eden.

The Black Canyon
of the Gunnison

As we descend the face of the cliff
   We travel at the edge of time,
Down and down to the
   Liquid center of the earth,
Down a layered history, past
   Dinosaurs and poisoned air,
Past discontented continents
   Jockeying for a better position
On the surface of a planet,

Mountains rising and eroding,
   Glaciers forming and receding,
Nature, never quiet,
   Never satisfied,
Evolving in error and haste.
   Correcting, congealing, at leisure
Forgetting, mercifully, the
   Distant light in the sky
Hurtling earthward thru space.

Before Poets

The hordes of Genghis Khan
    And Tamerlane,
As they marched westward across
    The endless steppes and muted valleys,
Did they remark on the beauty
    Of rolling foothills or shifting dunes,
Or gaze on the glory of the Asian
    Mountains, the spring flowers,
The sibilant pines?

At night did they watch in awe
    A sky backfilled with clouds
Illuminated with all the colors
    Of the spectrum by
A sun reaching for the night horizon?

Did they give thanks for the oases
    In the clefts of the earth,
The watering holes in the desert
    Beneath the vertiginous fronds
Of the palms or the sheltering
    Leaves of the dates?

Did they remark on the distance
    Traveled for the day and the distance
Yet to go? Did they know?

Were there no poets or scribes
    To count the days
To measure the nights,

But only beastly warriors
    Intent on pillage and death,
Smelling of sweat and feces
    And the blood of virgins?

Trees

It is said that trees talk
  To each other.
I wonder what they say.
    Do they gossip about the
Proud nudity of oaks and maples
    In winter,
About the never ceasing
    Murmuring of the pines?
    "Are they never quiet?"
The endless squatting of birds,
    "…You can't evict them…"
Bugs, bugs, the itch, itch,
    The nibbles on leaves,
The gnawing on the bark,
    The moss and lichen
In the crotch
    Of the branch where you
    Can't scratch?
Apples? "They never fall
    far you know…"

"And who knows what the
   weather will be?"

Do they worry that the distracted
   Communism of the forest
Will attract the settlers
   And the lumberjacks
Who will bring with them
   A clear world of straight
Lines and silenced plants.

Zero

Before infinity and zero from the east
    You could put a lid on the world,
Keep it in a box
    Locked by popes and saints.

And on the upper stories
    Angels and old souls dwelt,

While down below the furnaces
    Of hell burned in the basement.
The first family had lit the flame.

But then the world turned upside down
    In an earthquake of abstractions.
Who knew that the key to all
    The knowledge in the world
Was contained in that
    Simple circle representing nothing?

Sound

Sound is nothing more than the
   Crests of hills and the floors of valleys,
A line traced in frequency,
   Linear, one dimensional in scope.
And yet, mapped from an atlas of those
   Scoped lines
Emerges the landscape of Vivaldi's
   Seasons.
The magic flight of the Firebird
   And the pastoral symphony
Of a deaf musician.

And those tracings melt from linear
   To liquid, a bubbling chain of
Notes that spill like fresh
   Milk from a pail,
Warm, succulent and nourishing.

The Great War

One definition of insanity is doing the same thing
Over and over and expecting a different result.
Thus may we see the great war in Europe
As a mass psychotic event,
A daily expectation of a new result,
With the only variance, by nightfall,
The number of dead or dying.

As the days and weeks and months went on
The minds of the generals hardened,
The psychoses endured.
No sliver of reason was allowed to creep
Into the dream turned nightmare of a plundered world.

One has to ask…
Why it never occurred to anyone on either side of the line
To call a truce, stop time,
Bring a hundred men, a thousand men, all the men,
From both sides on the battered trench
To build a fence for the hours,
Mark a point and hold, momentarily, violence at bay.

And then to bathe the soldiers, wash away the blood and soil,
The stink of war,
And send them home for just a day,

To hold son or infant daughter and feed them
From a tiny spoon by a flame-warmed hearth.
To hold mothers close and kiss their worry-wrinkled brows,
To smoke a cigarette, light a pipe with wizened grand-peres.

To sing a hymn in church, buy a flower,
Pick a bean from the kitchen garden,
Take a wife to bed and love her long.
Be silent as the dawn.

And the next morning, decide whether or not
The spell of war has passed, the fever broken
And leave the fence in the cratered field.

Defenseless

When we were young children
    Our parents didn't want us to have toy guns
Or other little weapons of minor destruction.
    But it is in the nature of children
To want to arm themselves.
    So from tree branches and binder twine
We fashioned bows and from soft pine
    Trimmed pointed arrows
With chicken feather fletchings and hollowed nocks;
    Arrows that flew neither straight, nor true
But flew nevertheless.

It is also in the nature of children
    Not to build cities but to build forts
And so we did in the old bank barn;
    Forts of straw and stiff oak planks
With tunnels and towers and bridges
    Across beams from which we could
Fall to an early glorious death.

Then, in secret, we carved rifles from
    Softer woods,
Established an encampment beyond the
    Picket fence and
Lay in wait for an enemy from beyond
    the horizon.

And right we were to fear invasion,
    For one evening, our father,
Looking for his canvas tarpaulin
    To cover new baled hay,
Tore our tent from its poles,
    Uprooted its pegged ends from the soil
And cursing, drug it off to
    Cover a mere load of clover,
leaving us at the mercy of the invading hordes.

Atoms

It should not surprise us
   That words and music
Can be reduced to strings
   Of ones and zeros
Or squiggles on a plastic plate,

That Beethoven's Ode to Joy,
   Mozart's Don Giovanni,
Can be pressed onto vinyl,
   Or stored on a chip the
Size of the tiniest insect
   In a thin rectangle of shiny metal.

Because in the end,
   All we are and all we see,
Are merely a collection of
   Brightly colored
Positives and negatives,
   Centrifuges spinning longingly
In the grasp of gravity.

Writing

Words no longer spill from
    Pens
But clatter onto a screen
    In hurried pixels,
And instead of lingering
    There for history or an
Untellable future,
    They melt away with
Just a touch,
    Taking with them
Memories.

It is known that writing,
    Real writing,
With pen or leaden pencil,
    Builds bridges and
Little waypoints
    In the brain,
Way stations
    Of love or care
Or just concern.

While pixelated
    Consonants
And vowels slide
    Smoothly over the
Surface of our knowing
    Leaving barely a trace.

A Duty of the King

Were I the King of England,
   (I dare not say Queen, lest confusion reign)
And the Earl of Merioneth,
   I would relish this Earlship above all
And spend my mornings on horseback
   Seeing over the lands and words of Wales.

Historic county, north by west, Merionethshire
   Quickly defined, and placed
In the rugged geography of an island;
   Perhaps it is this very ruggedness
That called for soft, sliding words
   Stuffed with enough consonants
To beckon souls and sheep to
   The slopes and bays

I would ride from the Eden and
   Wnion valleys into Snowdonia
And the Berwyn mountains, thinking
   On Gwynedd and Derbyshire.
I would ride through the Bala cleft,
   Find the gravestone of Merion and his
Granddad Cunedda, visit Glendower's
   Parliament town of Dolgellau,
And think on Glyndyfrdwry for a while.

25

Bounded to the north by
    Caernarfonshire,
To the east by
    Denbighshire,
And to the west by
    Cardigan Bay,
Need I say more?

But, of course, I must, since
    I am King, and Kings rule
From Mountain tops, low may
    They be on this fair green isle.
But I shall put a throne on
    Cadair Idris and take a morning rest
While my horse grazes,
Sit a while at Arenig Fawr,
    Take morning tea on
An old oak table at Rhinogydd,
    Take some selfies at
The Dyli and the Dee to show
    Camilla in the afternoon.
(Or perhaps not, not Kingly
    after all.)

Late morning, I must peer at
  Waterfalls, see Pistyll
And Cain, and stand on the
  Shores of Bala Lake.

At noon, I shall ride my steed
  Back to a royal pub
And dash off a note to the
  President of France,
Challenging him to
  A pronunciation contest.

The Big Bang

It took a long time to develop
    My own explanation of the big bang,
And how so much could have
    Been created in such a short time.

I'm not suggesting an alternate
    Physics, mind you;
So do not submit this paper
    To a jury of my peers.

But rather, think of it as no more
    Outrageous than the book
Of Genesis
    With several billion man-years
Condensed into a day.

If we assume that light was
    Born in that instant, then
Time, that had just begun,
    Must equally have had to
Stop,
    at that velocity,

And all is but an illusion,
    Waiting for light to slow
So that time may begin to leak
    Into the future.

Birdsong

It is said that listening to birds
   Chirping and singing is good
For your mental health,
    That it connects you to nature,
      Distances you from yourself
        And your petty narrow world;
That it stimulates a better part
   Of your brain than the part that
     Gossips idly and follows electronic
Flickers as if they bore a truth
   From a holy mountain
     Instead of base commercial fictions.

That it relieves stress, expands your horizon
   And teases with a taste of long-lost freedom.

That is all likely to be true,
   For a single visit to a dinosaur museum
    Will show you the hollow bones
Of Archaeopteryx, the Ur Vogel,

And the deep reptilian portion of your brain
   Will remember the time before the comet,
And you will understand that these
   Are soulmates flitting about your backyard.

Or at least, that's what my
   Inner dinosaur believes.

The Flight of a Big Bird

This morning, I saw a great brown owl glide
   Silently from the branch of one large oak tree
To the branch of another.

The glide path of the owl traced the shape
   Of the base of a pair of heart-shaped
      Roller coaster loops,
A shape that can be explained by a
    Complex mathematical formula
      That looks like calculus but probably isn't.

But for me, I was, for a brief moment, back
   In the age of dinosaurs in the primordial forest,

And based on the cacophony of terrorized
   Warnings from the songbirds and squirrels
    In the neighboring trees,
So were they.

Deus Ex Machina

There is a certain sadness to a plane that will never fly again,
Its rudder frozen, instruments blind and windshield
Crazed and dusty,
To an engine that will never turn again,
Pistons seized to cylinder walls, never to feel
The sparking joy of power again,
To a tractor rusting in a field, tires brittle and flat,
Seat drooping, steering bent, and the hood
Home now to the occasional bird or bee
To the algaed boat, half sunk, lying in shallows
Or storm-tossed on a hostile shore,
Dismasted and forlorn.

Machines do not have souls.

But don't tell me that there is no difference
In spirit between a plane soaring above
A wash of clouds
And the sad fuselage by the hangar wall.

Between the rusted motor and the revving
    Of a low-slung car.

Between the now dead tractor and one pulling
    A plow over a spring-green field.

And between the sunken hulk and
    A sloop tacking across an emerald bay.

Machines do not have souls.

Perhaps it is all a matter of definition.
    Less sacredness, more busy-ness.

The Moon

Without the moon, this moon, the
   Very one we have today
It is probable that the earth
   We have today, this earth,
The very one we have today,
   Would not be green and moist
And fair.

For once upon a time, the
   Oceans were filled not
With water but a devil's
   Brew of elements and acids
That washed at the speed
   Of a hurricane against a
Hostile shore.

At that time, our moon, the
   Very one that hangs
In the sky, the
   Moon whose mother earth
Calved her,
   Was loath to leave the cradle
And she circled near,
   Nearer than today, driving
Those acrid tides against
   The early beaten shore,

And from that ceaseless storm
    Emerged a new element,
Benign to us but deadly to
    The past and
The atmosphere was born.

But now, a job well done,
    A tired moon, our moon,
Battered, cratered, lifeless,
    Must gaze jealously at
What it wrought, and
    Resentfully, slowly, drift away

The Ark

When I lived in Africa it rained
One season for more than
Forty days and forty nights.
And the water ran down
From the hills into the valleys
And the swamps
And then on down into the
Streams and rivers.
The rivers rose between their banks
And flowed deep and brown
Down to the coastal plains
And lowlands
Where the water spread out
Into great seasonal lakes
And marshes, and rested there.

Until the dry season, when
These lakes slowly drained
Into the ocean and
Left a layer of new rich
Soil, leached and torn
From the highlands.

And never once, no matter how
Long or how hard it rained
Did the water ever threaten
To drown the villages or cover
The hills or the upland forests.

So I wonder about the ark
  And the mountain and the
Dove with the olive branch.
I think they got it wrong,
  God's scribes.

I think there was a little legend,
  A tale told late at night
By a warming fire in a cold cave,
  Or by mighty river,
  A simple harvest tale
A tale of birth and death,
  Of dearth and plenty,

And as legends will do, it grew,
  And instead of a tale of
Richness restored to a parched
  Field by a benevolent god,
A tale of a bounty of fish,
  A rich harvest of nuts and roots,
A herd of antelope for the taking,

It became a cautionary tale,
  Perhaps to frighten children,
Perhaps to forestall greed,

Or maybe wishful thinking,
  Driven by envy or lost lands,
A plea to an evolving god
  For a clean slate, a fresh start.

Spring

There is no true fellowship with
Such a fickle season
Brittle broken promises
Of birth and bright flowers

Pale death beneath the
Bridal white of frost
An insidious chill over
An impatient landscape

Summer, 1954

The sky descends and under
    Pressure, we grow hot.
The land bakes, plant cells curl,
    Survival is the theme
Of the drawn-out day.

At night the Northern lights
    Steal south into the
Vacuum,
    But they retain their
Dancing chill
    And we swelter still
In silence.

Autumn

The moon comes closer to the earth,
    To survey the gathering, the dying leaves
    And clear clean skies filled
With birds that descend and blacken
    Fields of newly sown wheat and barley,
To reap an early harvest.

How many millions of birds,
    These plundering raptors from the skies,
    To find the millions of seeds, the millions
Of tiny roots from damp-sprouted kernels.
    To feed on them,

And then at evening, signaled by the dying
    Light, they fly in clouds as dense as
    Fog back to the foothills of the mountains
And perch on limb and branch, only
    To awaken with the new dawn
And continue the daily pillage until
    The fields are bare or the leaning of
The earth calls them south.

We used to stare at them in awe and
   Anger, wishing them to go away.
And now they have,

 And the autumn skies
  Are empty, the fields clear,
And we are poorer for it.

Winter

The furnace ran only enough to
  Keep the pipes from freezing,
Unless the pastor came for
  Sunday dinner, or someone died.

We slept under mounds of quilts
  And bathed weekly in the
Clawfoot tub, in a bathroom
  Warmed by an electric heater.

We woke to frosty windows,
  Cold floors and a stove not
Yet lit, weak sunlight struggling
  Over the mountains to
The east, an empty meadow
  And plumes of smoke
From new-kindled fires in
  Other cold kitchens by the way.

It was your own fault if
  You looked at the thermometer
On the outside wall;
  You would then no longer be able
To kid yourself that maybe winter
  Would be taking a break today
And the holes in your gloves
  Wouldn't matter.

Hell

What a terribly disorganized place,
  A management nightmare,
Until Dante came along and sorted
  It into seven circles.

Which I would argue, is not enough.
  There are many schools of thought
On how to run a place, even one
  Like hell. I'll admit to seven
Deadly sins, but are there not sins less
  Awful, deserving a little less time than
Eternity in this bureaucratic swamp?

And do the minor devils get monthly reviews,
  Compensation based on the rate
Of inflation or the price of coal for the
  Fires, the number of souls dispatched,
Or the sharpness of their spears?

Of course, in the end, if it took
  A poet to bring order to the place,
I suppose there is little hope
  Of instituting principles of
Management and a good set of books.

Fireflies

There were once two firmaments.
   Of equal nightly brightness over
The wheat gold fields of summer,
   The upper fixed, eternal,
Elemental, infinite, a glossary of
   Heavenly superlatives.

But the lower was a dance
   Of skittering blinking lights,
A layer of the atmosphere
   Shimmering above the heads
Of ripening grain, more
   Finite, more vulnerable
Then we knew.

They are mostly gone now,
   The lightning bugs,
Known to the Ancient Greeks
   As *Kysolampis,*, the beetle with
The shining buttocks,
   Photuris Pennsylvanica
Of the *Lampyridae* family;
   In the larval stage a glowworm.

We poisoned them in the name
  Of bread and cattle feed,
Killed them off, these harmless
  Flashing bugs, and now,
We have cold satellites
  Roaming the skies as
The stars, fleeing, send back
  A chilly filtered light.

A Modern Grace at Dinner

Dear God, Heavenly Father, Savior
  Of the exceptional,
Thanks for dinner and the kind hands,
  Willing or un, that prepared it.
Thanks for the migrant workers
  Who planted it, sprayed it,
Picked it and packed it,
  For the giant corporation that
Labelled it, shipped it and
  Sent profits to its shareholders.
For the drive-thru window
  With touchless payment in
A bright garish box of glass, steel
  And plastic, from which it emerged,
Hot, fat-full, caloric and
  Microwaved to its own
Standard of perfection.

Amen

The True Life of Birds

It says in the Bible that the birds of the air
   And the beasts of the field need not toil
Or sweat,
   That the great provider sees to their every
Need and that their lives are effortless.

When, in fact, birds are the workaholics of
   The animal world (I can't say the same of beasts.)
Birds hunt, pluck, peck, gather, build, and transport.
   They commute thousands of miles, navigate
By stars, entertain us with bright colors
   And endless song, and teach their young.

So, I'm just wondering, if the early authors
   Of the Bible got this so wrong, what
Else did they miss?

Flight

It has taken, it seems,
A hundred years of flight
To understand a bird,
The strength of hollow bones,
The grace of the sculpted wing,
The piercing dive of the
Noble hawk,
The magic lift of hot air
Over brown fields
As kettling raptors
Circle skyward in silence.

Now we know that
We will never flap
A wing to rise about the earth
And will never purchase
Space with feathered arms,
But must ever spoil the
Air with sound and great
Fury to obtain the worlds
Of clouds and ancient gods.

No Square Stars

If you look at the night sky
　Or more correctly, when you used to
Be able to look at the night
　Sky, and actually see a star,
Before streetlights, night lights
　Bug lights, stoplights, airplane light
And satellites, back a millennium
　Or three, in a world lit only by
Dim fires and a seasonal moon,

When the sky was a dark mysterious
　Place filled with the wash of the
Milky way, a few planets posing as
　Stars, and when the moon was
Idling away on the other side of the earth
　And not dominating the
Celestial conversation,

You might see a thousand or two,
　And maybe like the Greeks, you'd
Name a few and turn them into
　Gods and beasts and a spider,
Or a crab or whatever happened
　To tickle your fancy
In that faraway, dark and private realm.

And might not it occur to you, that stars,
  Like the moon that hides each month,
Are all round, the moon indisputably so,
  With those sharp brazen curves that
Slice the night and blank your gods and
  Beasts, your goddesses and crabs.

Not forgetting the sun, also round, but
  Too dangerous to observe, too
Hot to trust, too unreliable, needing to be
  Coaxed back to life each morning,
Demanding youth and virgins on
  Stone altars

And might you not then ponder the earth
  Beneath your feet, and considering
That you can never reach the horizon
  No matter how far you walk,
Wonder if it might also be round
  And not the flat dusty disc
That your elders propound, with
  An edge that must surely
Fall to an endless depth?

But if human nature is true,
  And observing the price of
Breaking tribal rules,
  You most likely kept those
Thoughts to yourself,
  Lest you be offered up
On one of those stone mounds
  A little burning light, a reminder
To think on gods, crabs
  And beasts.

The Last Spy

The last spy on earth decides to pen
  His own epitaph, a history of his own.
Lest a lesser soul be tasked with
  Tracing his deeds, good, bad and some
Unknown.

To count his crossings, double or sometimes not,
  Over borders, hills and plains, on foot,
By air, and once across a dessert, with a maiden
  Lank and fair.

For you to know, that his lies
  And guns were merely tools of trade,
That he meant no harm to
  Innocents, or innocence, and hopes
He did not often fail.

Yes, he wants all to know, he did not
  Want to work in vain,
That coded letters, micro-dots
  And anti-truths will help explain,
The duties felt to god and land,
  To fellow spies, his tight-knit clan.

And that the buried bodies
  And the grieving girls, now
Beyond knowing and caring still,
  Will soon find rest.

Mozart and Cicadas

The low hills beyond the Rhone,
    Dry summer, the mistral
Has passed. Wind-stressed
    Trees now stand still,
Resting in the noonday sun.
    On the branches
Cicadas plunk at sound
    With their click buzz,
click buzz and slide,
While under the arbor
    Mozart's flute skips
Over notes written for
    Light air and teased
Leaves, and the green
    Grapes on the vine,
While in the background
    Figaro waits.

The Problem with Greek Gods

The gods of ancient Greece
Were like the royal houses
   Of Europe.
It is very difficult to remember
   Who married whom for
What reason,
   Who mistook whom to
Be loyal,
   Who slept with whose
Maid, sister, or worse.
   Who hoped to gain an
Empire, new legions
   Of warriors, a new
Bride.
   Who hoped, through birth,
To dominate a world,
   Vanquish a pope,
A jealous rival god.

Who swore false oaths
  To weld a union,
Only to sunder with
  A sword, an axe,
The inconvenient head,
  Or lock in exile
The handsome suitor,
  Chastity preserved, wills
Broken, and the ember of
  Vengeance stoked in
A now hardened breast.

What battles fought
  On the sea, in the
Imaginary air of gods and
  goddesses,
In the desert south of
  The shore of the
Known world,
  Or the mudded plain
Of the last empire
  On earth.

The Smell of War

I have read that in the
Second half of the second
  Decade of the
Twentieth century,
  When two large armies,
(I will not call them great)
  Sent daily, thousands of
Men, a few horses,
  And tons of ammunition
To their bitter ends
  In a slaughtered land,
With nothing gained
  But bloodied bones
And a need for wood
  For the coffin maker's hand,
That you could smell the
  War, the stench of death,
The reek of waste
  For miles away.

I have read as well, that
  In the city-states of
The Italian renaissance,
  The time of knowledge new
And art upon the walls,
  When the earth began
To move around the sun
  And gravity found

Its true pull,
  A time when nobles,
Given to learning and
  Avarice, and popes,
Given to avarice alone,
  Hired armies, mercenary,
Unkempt, roving battalions
  To fight their battles,
Defend their greed,
  And oft as not, plunder
And despoil,

That, as in time
  To come,
Five centuries on,
  When learning had stood still,
You could sense these
  Fetid warriors from far away,
And know the smell of war.

The Bobcat

Years before my birth, a lone
  Bobcat came to the valley
And haunted the hedgerows
  And verges of the farmers' fields.
It climbed trees and rested
  On limbs and thought
Of rabbits and small children.
  It lived wild, untamed,
Out of its element, lost to
  The hills of the distant range.
It roamed at night,
  Slept at dawn in a place
Unknown to man.
  It spread terror, brought
Trembling to women's knees,
  Caused the world to
Lock its doors, and farmers
  To carry guns.

Or so my grandpa said.
  No one ever saw the cat,
No one ever died, but
  Sure were all of the
Beast at large, and
  The tale was carried on.

The legend never died, so
  On cold winter nights,
When it was my turn
  To walk the dark path
To the silent, sleeping barn,
  To check the cows now fed,
I wondered in fear,
  Which night would
Bring my end; when the
  Hungry cat would come
At last, leap from
  The shadows and
Finally, sate a hunger
  Borne of decades gone
And rumors lost.

Sennacherib

Only seven times a dozen years,
   Your city by the Tigris reigned,
Largest city of the old, old world.

Your palace a thousand cubits long
  And half as many wide,
Fifty cubits to the ceiling, or more,
  One and a half million bricks of mud,
Eighty rooms, the history of evil
  Engraved upon the walls and
Statues the weight of a hundred men.

This palace, built on the bank of
  The great river, the giver of life
At Nineveh, the last port for
  Ships up from the sea.

It is no wonder that your palace
  Did not last, built on too much
Blood, death and suffering.
  The Babylonians, gladly left to
Rot in the streets of the ravaged city,
  The dead of Jerusalem, walled
Off to waste and die.

And you, dead at the hands of
   Your own two sons.

There is only so much evil
   That a place can take,
And should God not have time
   To put this right, some King,
Some priest, some righteous
   Man, perhaps,
Will see your kingdom to its
   Death, despoil your palace,
And send it crumbling
   To the dust.

Holofernes

Well bud, you really screwed the pooch this time,
   You really lost your head over a hot chick,
Well, hardly a chick, seeing as how she's a widow.
   But, hot, nevertheless, in so many ways.
And you, on the verge of invading home and hearth,
   Might ought to keep in mind who you're inviting into your tent,
Or whose inviting you to hers, (especially when it's her
   Home and her hearth, you and the horde are about
To pillage. No?)

So, typical, you guys are all the same, sex trumps all,
   And how much wine *did* you drink, before you
Tumbled from the bed, lust unquenched?
   Were you so drunk, you didn't wonder, when
The maid came into the gloom? Did you think this would
   Be a desert threesome play?
Well, there were three of you for sure, one to aid
   In holding, one to wield the knife, and neither one
Of those was you.

Did you feel the blade, as it sliced your throat?
   Did you have time to utter Judith, curse her name?
Well, doesn't matter now. Your head is on a platter,
   And the rest of you drug off as a further reminder,
That there are some places you ought not to invade.

The Motorcycle

Picture this, a dark moonless night,
   early winter, surely past eleven,
a small country road
   that leads from one small
town to another by way of
   a minor settlement or two,
and crossing one river,
   two streams and a mill race
filled with mud.
   Two crossroads and at
neither, does this little road
   have right of way.
Before one crossroad there
   are two sharp turnings and
a small bridge.
   And at this crossroad there
stands a small house,
   dark and now silent, the
oil heater turned low
   for the night.

In this house, a boy of ten
   is awakened by the noise of a
motorcycle as it makes
   the second of the turns
and accelerates toward the
   stop sign by the house.

He holds his breath,
  as the motorcycle shows
no sign of slowing, but
  instead seems to be gaining
speed, the stop sign surely
  in his sights by now.
It is coming ever faster
  and there will not be time
to brake, should a car or
  truck be passing on the
other road.

In the boy's mind, nothing
  is right about this,
this challenge to all good
  sense and all good order.
This is not what men
  and boys do, this is the
stuff of demons and legends,
  of challenged norms, of
death ignored and worlds
  torn apart.
This is wrong and he
  expects the crash,
only to hear the motorcycle
  accelerate further as it climbs
the hill beyond the house
  and disappears over the crest
of the hill in the dark.

It was me who was woken
    that night and I can still
hear the motorcycle as it guns
    its way through the intersection,
feel a surge of fear-based
    adrenalin, a prickling of the skin.
And when I thought, those
    many years ago, of demons
and legends, I was not
    wrong I think,
for did this not become the
    stuff of this small legend
to live on in these few words?

Nineveh

You know, it takes a pretty
  good agent to get your name
in the first book of the Bible.
  (Or a little honey or mead
slipped to the scribe.)
But there you are, not long after
  Eden, which of course, *was*
only a garden, with a bad
  reputation, as it turns out,
So maybe getting the largest
  city in the world mentioned
in Genesis isn't all that big a
  deal after all.

But me, being of a suspicious
  nature, find it interesting
that Mesopotamia, the land
  between the rivers
just happens to be where
  your town popped up.
Mesopotamia, the place where
  civilization as we know it,
with farms and fields, and
  cultivation and the new
obligation of all that hard
  work, took root.

So, if we could step back
  in time, and have a quick
word with the chamber of
  commerce, or your
publicity agent, might it be
  that Nineveh did a little
name change after you
  closed down the orchard in
town with the nudist colony
  after you had a problem
with snakes?

French Cicadas

At seven forty-five each evening,
   in July, the cicadas pick up
their little buzz saws and
   go down the trunk to the local
bar for a glass of cricket rosé
   or whatever cicadas drink.
I'm sure it's in their union
   contracts to take this break.
Later in the evening the
   night shift will come on and a
few soloists warm up
   here and there as the sun
goes down.

So, it got me to thinking
   about the seventeen-year
locust, and knowing the
   retirement benefits in
France, I would guess
   that their contract was
negotiated just after the war
   when things were in
turmoil, there was a temporary
   shortage of cicadas,
and no one read the fine print.

And now, when their excessive
  leave time comes up every
seventeen years, by the time
  parliament debates it and
proposes a solution, it's too late.
  The cicadas head back
down to locust central, arrange
  for a wake-up call,
make sure their pensions stay
  in long-term government
bonds, and go back to sleep.

Borromeo

Cardinal Federico, of the family Borromeo,
  With an offer you were not allowed
To refuse, at the age of twenty-three,
  To be Cardinal.
You demurred, but no, the pope would
  Not have it, for you of great means,
So you accepted, and to this day, a part
  Of the western world has gained from it.

The books of deeds are filled with
  Conquest, wars and woe, inbred
Dreams of noble houses, Kings in diapers,
  And dark princes of evil.
So much so, that a tale of a good man
  Is a rare thing.

And the story of your life, your deeds,
  Is a marvel, a man who fed two
Thousand people a day in the times
  Of plague, acted with humility and
Lived a life of grace.

More, a man who built the great library,
    The Biblioteca Ambrosiana, with its school
For languages, and books along the walls,
    Not chained to desks, trapped knowledge
Available only to priests, scribes and the learned.
    Books, tomes, manuscripts for any who
Could read, in Latin, Greek, Italian.

And even more, books from Germany, Greece
    Lebanon, and Jerusalem, from Flanders,
France and Spain. And the languages to
    Be taught, the languages of gods and seers,
Hebrew, Chaldean, Arabic, of Persia and
    Armenia. The study of Islam, of Judaism,
All, allies in the counter-reformation.

But in your heart, there dwelt a dark place,
    Drawn to witchcraft and the occult,
And you had nine witches flayed and burned,
    Torture beyond belief and normal pain.

And did you not hide away your friend,
    The author of your works, whose intellect
You passed off as your own. A ghost-writer,
    Banished to a dark, quiet cell?

How to balance lies and the dark arts
  Against the feeding of the poor,
How to measure murder, the abandonment
  Of Christ, against the priestly vows,
How to credit tolerance, for Mohammed
  And the Jews, how to honor knowledge,
Against the burning pyre.
  You served God, is forgiveness due,
And at the end, did you think on it and weep?

Mesopotamia

We must, of necessity, be drawn to this most
   Violent geography, there is no stasis.
Neither the people nor the land can settle,
   For your history is longer than we know.
We must cast our eyes and thoughts back
   Ten thousand years and more, when the earth
Lay frozen and the hungry ice had drained the
   The seas, connected islands, and laid bare
The windblown shore.

Did your rivers, roving through a shallow plain,
   Run cold and barren, until the ice gave up
Its hold, and the sea, the sea rose,
   To those abandoned shores, and spread
To the gates of Eden; Eden, long ago cursed
   And Cain justly sent to wander in the dust?

Or were you the true Ark?
   Snow is water of a different
      Form.
Was the flood, not of water,
   But of glaciers thick enough
      To crush the earth.
Did Ararat, not so far distant,
      Emerge from the ice, the snow,
And a white dove
      Flutter from the
New warm marsh?

The great melt brought the sea to your door.
   It reclaimed a rightful place and,
At its peak, six thousand years ago,
   Opened you to the world anew.

Born of this new world, Ur, now a city by the sea,
   Birthplace of tongues and poets,
Stratified, coded, King and Priest, Farmer,
   Fisherman, Builder, Slave.

Emerging from dry solitude to harvest
   The rich bounty of the marsh, the fish from
The now warm sea, who among you formed
   The first wheel, who carved the Standard
Of war and chariots backed up to peace
   And the marketplace of normal life?
Who dug canals, built the great mound,
   The Ziggurat; recorded the tablets of
Deeds, poems and daily bread?

Did Inanna, daughter of Nanna, God of
   Moon and Wisdom and she, Priestess of Love,
Sensuality, Fertility, Procreation and War,
   Guide you to this new civilization, or was it
The curse of Eden, coming to bear on man and beast?

Or were you driven by the fickle sea, once again
   Receding over the eons? Did the land rise?
Was the God of the Harvest jealous of the God of the Sea?

For slowly the land did rise, trapping your great
    Cities of Nineveh and Ur. Was the opening
To the world too much?

    You were the beating eastern heart of the
Old Testament, the beginning of life, the
    Beginning of death, the
Forecast of eternal consequences.
    Did you, like Icarus, dare too far?
Did the Tower, reaching to the sky, displease
    The Gods, who tore your peoples' words
From them and cast them like chaff, to
    The four corners of the world?

Is it in the nature of man to destroy
    All that he has built?
Did your indifference to a smooth
    Passage of time,
Or simple greed, rend
    The new fabric?
All cities rise from the mud and,
    Time passing, crumble into dust,
Just as the hungry land rewrote your shore.

Enheduanna

Who are you Enheduanna?
    Why don't we know you better?
Who are you Enheduanna?
    You, high priestess, rudely dethroned
    By a Sumerian imposter.
Who are you Enheduanna?
    First woman poet of all time,
    First woman, indeed, first person, to write
    "The compiler of this tablet is Enheduanna."
Who are you Enheduanna?
    Denied by men this title of first author,
    First to claim the right to tell the story.

But you will not be denied, you,
    High Priestess of the moon goddess
    Inanna; you, daughter of Sargon, beholden to none.
Charged with melding the Gods of Sumer and
    Akkad, Gods of field, fertility and war.

You, whose psalms, your psalms, daughter to the
    Psalms of the Testament and poems of Homer.
You: exiled, offended, demeaned by the invader,
    You held fast, implored Inanna, who answered,
And restored you to your rightful high place.

But who should marvel at this feat.
    If you could tame two worlds of gods, make
A country kneel to the religion of the state?
    Then Inanna owed you a recompense,
A godly due.

Glossary

Akkad. Probably the first ancient empire of Mesopotamia (c.2334–2154 BC) following the Sumerian Period. (See Sumer)

Black Canyon of the Gunnison. Deep Canyon west of Gunnison, Colorado, whose steep walls give exposure to two million years of rock formations dating back to the Precambrian age.

Borromeo, Federico. Cardinal appointed Archbishop of Milan in 1595 by Pope Clement VIII. Noted for founding the Biblioteca Ambrosiana as described in the poem, to promote the Catholic response to the Reformation and for his generosity with inherited family fortune.

Enheduanna. High Priestess of the moon god Nanna in the Sumerian city-state of Ur (c.2334–2379 BC). First recorded author in history. Daughter of Sargon. (See Sargon of Akkad.)

Holofernes. Assyrian General dispatched, most likely by Nebuchadnezzar, to take vengeance on Israel (date not given). He laid siege to the town of Bethulia, but Judith, a Hebrew widow, got him drunk and beheaded him, saving the city.

Inanna. Mesopotamian goddess of love, war and fertility. Also known as Ishtar with the title of Queen of Heaven, by the Akkadians and the Sumerians. (See Akkad and Sumer.)

Nanna. Moon god in Mesopotamian region of Sumer and Akkad associated with power and cattle due to his horned appearance.

Nineveh. Capital and largest city of the Neo-Assyrian Empire and largest city in the world from c.660–612 BC. Across the river from present day Mosul in Iraq.

Sargon of Akkad. (2334–2279 BC). Founder of the Akkadian Empire. Father of Enheduanna. (See Enheduanna, Akkad.)

Sennacherib. Second King of the Sargonid dynasty in Mesopotamia from 705–681 BC. Famous in the Hebrew Bible for his role in the destruction of Babylon 689 BC.

Sumer. Earliest known civilization in Mesopotamia, now Iraq. (c.5500–1475 BC)

Ur. Important Sumerian city-state. Founded c.3800 BC. Now Tell el-Mugayyar, Iraq.

Zero from the east. Refers to Leonardo of Pisa, also known as Fibonacci, an Italian renaissance mathematician credited with bringing Arabic numerals to Europe around 1200 AD. Prior to that it was not possible to do complex mathematical calculations as there was no symbol for zero.

Ziggurat. Pyramidal stepped temple tower characteristic of major Mesopotamian cities.